Giving
Presentations

Pocket Mentor Series

The *Pocket Mentor* Series offers immediate solutions to common challenges managers face on the job every day. Each book in the series is packed with handy tools, self-tests, and real-life examples to help you identify your strengths and weaknesses and hone critical skills. Whether you're at your desk, in a meeting, or on the road, these portable guides enable you to tackle the daily demands of your work with greater speed, savvy, and effectiveness.

Books in the series:

Leading Teams
Running Meetings
Managing Time
Managing Projects
Coaching People
Giving Feedback
Leading People
Negotiating Outcomes
Writing for Business
Giving Presentations

Giving Presentations

Expert Solutions to Everyday Challenges

Harvard Business School Press

Boston, Massachusetts

No part of this publication may be reproduced, stored in or introduced into a re-trieval system, or transmitted, in any form, or by any means (electronic, mechanical, photocopying, recording, or otherwise), without the prior permission of the pub-lisher. Requests for permission should be directed to permissions@hbsp.harvard.edu, or mailed to Permissions, Harvard Business School Publishing, 60 Harvard Way, Boston, Massachusetts 02163.

Library of Congress Cataloging-in-Publication Data
Giving presentations : expert solutions to everyday challenges.
    p. cm. — (Pocket mentor series)
  Includes bibliographical references.
  ISBN 978-1-4221-1475-9 (pbk. : alk. paper)
  1. Business presentations. I. Harvard Business School Publishing
Corporation.
  HF5718.22.G58 2007
  658.4'52—dc22   2007000875

The paper used in this publication meets the requirements of the American National Standard for Permanence of Paper for Publications and Documents in Libraries and Archives Z39.48-1992

Contents

Prepare   19

Once you know your objective, it's time to organize your materials to fit the allotted time.

Plan for Visuals   27

Good visual aids will give your presentation impact, keep the audience engaged, and make your points stick.

When It's a Group Effort   35

When is it a good idea to use a group presentation? And what's the best way to integrate several people into a presentation?

Rehearse   39

Don't wing it! A rehearsal will improve your delivery and expose weaknesses in your presentation.

Prepare Yourself   43

As presenter, you need steady nerves and the right mental attitude.

Show Time   47

You will achieve your best performance if you speak effectively, project a positive image, and keep your audience engaged. But how do you do that?

How to speak effectively   48

Project a positive image   49

Techniques for keeping your audience engaged   49

Handling Questions   53

If you want to handle questions effectively, anticipate and prepare for likely audience queries.

The right time for Q&A   54

Prepare yourself for the tough questions   55

When you don't have the answer   57

After-Action Review   59

Good presentation skills are a career asset for managers. So treat every presentation as an opportunity for continual improvement.

Find the root causes of problems   60

A video can help   61

Tips and Tools   63

Tools for Giving Presentations   65

Worksheets that can help you prepare systematically.

Test Yourself   73

A helpful review of the concepts presented in this guide. Take it before and after you've read through the guide to see how much you've learned.

Answers to test questions   76

To Learn More   79

Titles of articles and books that can help you further master this topic.

Sources for Giving Presentations   83

Notes   85

Use this Notes section to record your ideas.

Mentor's Message: Clarify and Inspire

Making persuasive presentations isn't just a matter of passion and PowerPoint; it requires concrete skills that keep your audience engaged and involved. This Pocket Mentor will help you connect what you know about your subject with what your audience needs—in ways that clarify and inspire. It contains relevant information on how to

- Prepare an effective presentation customized for your audience and setting

- Deliver an effective presentation that produces action

- Address questions and keep people focused during your presentation

Good luck with your next presentation!

Nick Morgan, Mentor

Nick Morgan is a communications expert who has worked as a speech-writer, a public relations director, and a communications professor. Through his company, Public Words LLC (www.publicwords.com), he coaches executives and runs seminars on a range of communication issues. He has been editor of *Harvard Management Communication Letter*, has written hundreds of articles, and is the author of *Working the Room: How to Motivate People to Action Through Audience-Centered Speaking* (HBS Press).

Giving Presentations: The Basics

All About
Presentations

We rule the world by our words.

—Napoleon Bonaparte

A PRESENTATION CAN BE A powerful way to *communicate your message to a group and to engage in two-way dialogue. Managers use presentations to*

- Persuade listeners to take a particular course of action

- Convey information

- Provide a forum for discussion

- Find out how people are reacting to a situation or an idea

- Gain commitment

- Engage people in problem solving

Types of presentations

There are many types of presentations, each designed to meet specific needs. Here are some examples:

- **Sales.** Outlines the benefits and features of a product or service; gives listeners a reason to buy.

- **Product demonstration.** Shows how something works.

- **Persuasion.** Provides reasons to support an idea.

- **Status report.** Details the progress of a project, a task force, or an incentive program.

- **Business plan or strategy.** Sketches out what an organization plans to do next or articulates the company's goals.

Whatever your purpose, however, don't use a presentation to dump lots of detailed information on an audience. Audiences remember few details delivered through a presentation. You can use a presentation to inform an audience about a major change or initiative, but use written communication for the details. Thus, your purpose drives the type of presentation you choose. You also need to tailor your presentation to these factors:

- Size of the audience

- Formality of the situation

- Regularity of the meeting (one-time, occasional, frequent)

- Time of day and other particulars of the occasion

First
Things First

LIKE MOST ENDEAVORS, an effective presentation begins with focused thinking. This doesn't mean preparation, which comes next. Instead, you should think about the objective of your presentation, the audience, and the context for what you'll eventually present.

Define your objective

The objective of your presentation is the outcome you want—persuasion, discussion, buy in, feedback, or a sale. Your objective should drive the development of your presentation. Begin by asking yourself these questions: "What is the purpose of this presentation?" "What do I want my audience to do as a result?" More specifically, ask these questions:

- Do I want to inform, persuade, or sell?

- Do I want the audience to understand, learn, or take action? Note the difference between presenting a budget so that your audience understands it and presenting a budget so that your audience votes on it.

- Do I want commitment from the audience?

Later, you'll want to include examples, visuals, and details that will help you achieve your objective. Anything that is extraneous, distracting, or interfering should be omitted.

Your objective also helps you determine the following:

- Whether to give the presentation at all; another mode of communication—such as having lunch with key decision makers—may be more effective

- Whether to give it to this particular audience under these particular circumstances

- What to say and how to say it

- What the follow-up needs to be

- Possible objections

Know your audience

A presentation is an interactive dialogue between you and your audience. The better you understand your listeners, the more you can customize your presentation. Make sure that you can answer these questions:

- Is the subject controversial, familiar, or new (or a combination) to this audience?

- Who are they, and what is their relationship to your topic?

- How well informed are they about the subject? What do they need to know about it?

- What do they expect from your presentation?

- Are they accustomed to a certain type of presentation?

- What do they know about you? What more do they need to know? How do they feel about you?

- Why are they present? Are they there by choice or by requirement?

- Are they likely to be enthusiastic? Polite? Apathetic? Hostile?

- Are there any other obstacles, history, or expectations that you need to take into account?

NOTE: Whether you are playing a competitive sport, conducting a business negotiation, or making a presentation, the more you understand the people on the other side of the encounter, the greater the odds that you'll be successful. Don't take a shortcut around this important aspect of preparation.

You can use the "Audience Characteristics" worksheet to guide your analysis.

Understand your presentation's context

No presentation is made in a vacuum. The context of your presentation will play a major role in how it will be received, so be aware of the following issues:

- Is the situation formal or informal?

- When you present, will the audience have just finished eating, drinking, working, having a break, or doing something active? Will they be tired or alert?

- Who will speak before you? Who comes after you? How might this affect audience reaction?

- Are you the first or last speaker of the program? The day? The morning or afternoon?

- Are you expected to take questions or leave copies of your presentation?

- How much time will you have for the presentation? Can your message be delivered in that time?

- Will the physical setting of the presentation require you to adapt your talk?

- What control will you have over the physical environment?

NOTE: To make sure you've covered all the details of your presentation's context, use the "Logistics" worksheet.

To help you understand the context of your presentation, use the "Presentation Context" worksheet.

Audience Characteristics

Use this worksheet as you prepare your presentation.

Question	Notes
1. Who are your listeners, and what is their relationship to your topic?	
2. How well informed are they about the subject matter?	
3. What do they need to know?	
4. What are their expectations of the larger event? Of your presentation?	
5. What do they know about you? What else might they need to know?	
6. What is their opinion of you or the organization you represent?	
7. Are they attending by choice or by requirement?	
8. Are they likely to be receptive? Enthusiastic? Polite? Hostile? Apathetic?	
9. Are there other obstacles, history, or expectations that you need to take into account?	
10. What presentation techniques might best capture their attention and get your points across most effectively (e.g., demonstrations, personal stories, multimedia)?	

Logistics

Complete this worksheet prior to your presentation to confirm that you haven't forgotten any of the logistical details.

Presentation Topic	
Date	
Presenter(s)	
Presentation Location	
Meeting Coordinator and Phone Number	
Site Contact Person and Phone Number	
Number of People Attending	
Handouts	

Room Setup

☐ Auditorium   ☐ Horseshoe   ☐ Podium

☐ Classroom   ☐ Breakout Sessions   ☐ Stage

☐ Conference   ☐ Tables: Front, Side, or Back

☐ Other:

Equipment and Supplies

☐ Computer(s)   ☐ Extension Cord(s)   ☐ Video equipment/ VCR player and monitors

☐ Overhead Projector/ Spare Bulbs   ☐ Flip Chart/Tape/ Markers   ☐ Phone Line(s)

☐ Projection Table   ☐ LCD Projector   ☐ Microphone

☐ Other:

Other

Presentation Context

Use this worksheet to better understand the context of your presentation.

Question	Notes
1. Is the presentation formal or informal?	
2. When you present, will the audience have just finished eating, drinking, working, or doing something active?	
3. Who will speak before and after you? What do they plan to say?	
4. Are you the first or last speaker of the program? The day? The morning or afternoon?	
5. Are you expected to answer questions or leave copies of your presentation?	
6. How much time do you have for the presentation? Can your message be delivered in that time? If not, can it be adapted and still be effective?	
7. Will the physical setting of the room require you to adapt your presentation in any way?	

Decide What
to Say

Everything becomes a little different
as soon as it is spoken out loud.
—Hermann Hesse

O NCE YOU'VE THOUGHT through your objective, you must decide what it is you want to say to your audience. This isn't always easy. Have you ever experienced a situation in which you knew your objective (convince the boss to adopt your new product plan) but didn't know which combination of arguments, data, and examples would achieve that objective? If you answered yes, you're in good company.

Three stages

Usually, the easiest way to cut through the "what should I say?" block is to divide the task into three stages.

Stage 1. Define the key message: what you want people to remember and what action you want them to take. This message flows directly from your objective. You can have a number of supporting arguments, ideas, and facts, but only one key message.

Stage 2. Identify the arguments that support your message. Avoid excessive detail, but be sure to talk about more than *just* the facts. It is important to identify and address the emotional underpinnings of your message. Why should the audience care about it?

NOTE: Statements made without benefit of supporting argument or evidence are merely opinions, and opinions have little impact on an audience. Give your audience reasons to share your views or adopt a course of action.

Stage 3. Identify when it is important to get audience participation, reactions, agreement, or buy in.

Review and refine your ideas

After you have generated your initial set of ideas on what to say, you are ready to review and refine them. Consider the following:

- Is the key message you have selected really the most critical? Does it support the objectives of the presentation?

- Are the arguments you have marshaled understandable to all levels of your audience?

- Will your content convince the audience to agree with you?

- Are the logical connections explicit?

- What arguments need to be developed?

- What contrary arguments will you need to neutralize?

Then, if persuasion is your goal, ask yourself what else you can do or say that may persuade your audience. Effective persuaders use arguments that combine logic and emotion. Your persuasiveness is largely a product of your enthusiasm, credibility, and personal belief in the subject.

Remember to include only those details that will persuade. Extraneous details will distract listeners from what you want them to hear, process, and remember. If you are not sure about the impact of a point, leave it out.

Prepare

O NCE YOU HAVE A firm idea about what you want to say and the objective of your presentation, you're ready for the next important step: preparation. Here you'll organize your presentation into a format that fits within an allotted time.

Organize your presentation

Once you have the raw material for your presentation, you need to organize it. A well-organized presentation will make the audience's listening job as easy as possible, boosting the likelihood that you will accomplish your objective. In most cases, a presentation should be organized with an opening, a need or problem statement, a solution, and a call to action.

Good organization begins with a compelling *opening*. During the opening, use a *hook*—a comment, question, relevant story, statement, or example—to get your audience's interest and attention. Here's an example. Notice how the presenter interacts with the audience to capture its attention.

Presenter:

So we're gathered here to learn more about leadership transitions.

How many of you have transitioned into a new management role in the last year? . . . Well, that's perhaps a fourth of the audience. Maybe a little more.

And how many have had a new supervisor in the last year? . . . A third—or close to a half.

Okay. Let's see how many have either moved into a new role or had a new supervisor in the last two years . . . And that's pretty much everyone!

So you see, we all *are engaged in leadership transitions. And the more we can do to make these transitions successful, the better!*

You also use the opening to do the following:

- Define the purpose of the presentation.

- Establish your credibility. Ask yourself, "Which of my credentials will impress this particular audience?" and emphasize those. Or, if appropriate, have another person with authority or credibility introduce your presentation.

- Describe the importance of the topic for the audience: what's in it for them?

- Preview very briefly the main points to be covered.

The second part of your presentation is the *need* or *problem statement.* Here you should do the following:

- Make it clear to the audience why it should care about your message.

- Develop a clear need or problem that you and the audience will solve together.

- Incorporate relevant arguments, examples, and a variety of supporting material to sustain interest without distracting from the point.

- Involve the audience members by asking for their suggestions and addressing their needs and issues.

- Test acceptance by asking for feedback, if appropriate.

The third part of your presentation, the *solution,* makes it clear to the audience how you think the problem should be solved or the need satisfied. Here you will do the following:

- Help the audience visualize the benefits of the solution.

- Involve the audience in developing a path forward.

- Phrase your solution in terms of the audience's needs.

- Make sure the urgency of your solution matches the need.

To wrap up, you need a strong *call to action.* Here you will want to do the following:

- Reiterate the presentation's key message.

- Integrate your opening points into your closing comments.

- Recommend action.

- Suggest agreement.

- Obtain commitment or buy in.

- Provide closure.

Tips for Setting Up a Presentation

- Identify the presentation's objective. It will drive everything you do.

- Learn as much as you can about your listeners, their biases, and their expectations.

- Address your topic from the audience's perspective.

- Tailor your presentation to accommodate the context—the physical environment, time of day, and significant ongoing event that may affect your listeners.

How long should a presentation be?

Often, you must fit your presentation into a timetable developed by others. For example, you may be granted thirty minutes to deliver a sales presentation to a buyer. In other instances, you are in control of the timing, and you can determine the optimal length for your presentation. The following guidelines are helpful in both situations:

- Make the presentation as long as it needs to be to convey your key message clearly and completely.

- Make it only long enough to be clear and complete within the allocated time.

- It is better to make fewer points and make them well.

- If you do not have time to make a point clear or acceptable to your audience, save it for another presentation.

- Ending early is better than not completing the talk or rushing through the talk at the end.

- Plan on what to delete if your time is cut short.

- Allow time at the end for questions as a basic courtesy.

Need help in planning your presentation? Consider using the "Preliminary Planning" worksheet.

Preliminary Planning

Use this worksheet to help you plan the content of your presentation.

Topic

Requested by

Objectives

If your presentation is a success, what will be the immediate results?

Main Messages

What must the audience understand and remember from your presentation?

1.

2.

3.

4.

5.

Supporting Facts

What facts support your main messages?

Message 1

Message 2

Message 3

Message 4

Message 5

Plan for
Visuals

A s you organize, identify opportunities to use visuals to get your points across and make them stick in the minds of listeners. Everyone has a preferred learning style, but most people respond better to visuals than to the spoken word alone. Consider the following research findings:

- People gain 75 percent of what they know visually, 13 percent through hearing, and 12 percent through smell.

- A picture is three times as effective in conveying information as words alone.

- Words and pictures together are *six times as effective* as words alone.

Use visual aids to help your audience maintain attention and remember facts. Use them also to help people understand ideas, relationships, or physical layouts. Visuals can also be used as cues that you are moving to a new topic.

Remember, however, that when the audience is looking at a visual, it is not looking at you, so keep visuals to a minimum. And do not use word-heavy slides to act as an outline; instead, know your speech thoroughly.

Choose the appropriate media

You have many choices for your visuals, including overheads, computer-based slides, flip charts, and handouts. When selecting from among these media, you need to consider flexibility, cost, and appropriateness for your presentation.

Media pros and cons

Medium	Pros	Cons
Overheads	• Flexible • Easy to create • Can allow light in the room for continued eye contact • Good for both formal and informal situations	• Can be awkward putting up and switching between overheads • Old technology
Computer-based slides	• Easy to create, update, transport	• Do not always project clearly • Technology can break down, so you need to have a backup set of overhead slides
Flip charts	• Flexible • Easy to create • Encourage interaction	• Not effective for large groups • Difficult to transport
Handouts	• Useful for informal, short presentations • Provide a place for note-taking and a take-away for later reference • Can contain supplemental background information	• Can become the audience's focal point, distracting them from listening to you

What Would YOU Do?

The Doggie Backpack

EVERY YEAR, OSCAR AND his product management group introduce new products at a national conference for BestPet, Inc., a manufacturer of pet products. To prepare the company's 150-member sales force to promote new products to retail customers, the product line managers outline new product features and benefits.

This year Oscar and his group will announce an exciting new product: the Trail Hound, a "doggie backpack" for dogs to carry their food and water during hikes with their owners. The Trail Hound has an innovative new compartment system. Oscar needs to explain this feature clearly so that the sales reps can demonstrate it to customers.

Oscar is scheduled to deliver his presentation just after lunch. In the weeks before the conference, he begins preparing visuals that he hopes will deepen the sales reps' understanding of the new product and inspire them to sell it.

If you choose to use handouts, avoid distributing them during the presentation. It detracts from your presentation.

Effective visuals

Not all visuals enhance a presentation. If you're like most white-collar workers, you're probably familiar with "death by Power-Point"—presentations in which the speaker uses too many slides, uses visuals with confusing flow charts of boxes, arrows, feedback loops, and text, packs visuals border to border with text or images, or, worse, simply reads the text in the visuals.

To be effective, visuals should

- Be simple

- Use graphics, icons, and symbols to reinforce or communicate a concept

- Use key words, not full sentences

- Use only one concept and no more than six lines per slide or page

- Use only three to six ideas on each flip chart sheet

- Use color, where possible, but not excessively

- Use pictures where possible

- Use bullets, not numbers, for nonsequential items

- Use all-uppercase letters only for titles or acronyms

  .

To organize all the elements of your presentation, use the "Presentation Outline" worksheet.

Tips for Creating Visuals

- Use a single idea with no more than six lines per slide.

- Be selective with your words.

- Don't use vertical lettering.

- Use a maximum of two sizes of type per page.

- Use uppercase and lowercase letters. Use all-uppercase only for titles or acronyms.

Presentation Outline

*Use this worksheet to help you organize your content most effectively,
identify any visuals or support materials that will enhance your
presentation, and estimate the time you will need. You may have to revise your
content if it appears to exceed your time limitations.*

Your Content	Visuals/Support Materials	Time
Opening		
• State your purpose. • Preview your main points. • Make your audience want to listen.		
Body		
• Get across the main points of your presentation.		
Conclusion		
• Summarize your content. • Challenge the audience to take action.		

What You COULD Do.

Which kind of visual would be most compelling for Oscar's purpose? Here are a few possibilities:

- A one-page list of the top ten reasons the Trail Hound backpack is better than any competing doggie backpack. Oscar could hand out the list during his presentation.
- A flip chart with two or three easy-to-see diagrams demonstrating how the Trail Hound's compartment feature works.
- A computer-based slide with an image contrasting Trail Hound's new compartment system with its top competitor's, and including a bulleted list of several advantages of the Trail Hound system.

In the end, Oscar decides to create a computer-based presentation composed of word-and-picture slides. He also elects to provide audience members with handouts detailing the Trail Hound's important specifications as they enter the conference room.

When It's a Group Effort

OFTEN, YOU WANT other people to contribute to your presentation. You may be presenting the results of a group effort, or you may feel that their presence and experience will help you achieve your objective. Consider this example:

Samantha, leader of a new product development team, plans to make a presentation to senior management about the team's progress in developing a new line of heart-healthy frozen food entrees. She decides that a group presentation would be best because it will allow team members with recognized technical expertise to explain the details of their work. With that in mind, she organizes the presentation to include the following people:

- *Harold, the nutrition expert on the team. He will address the nutritional and medical issues faced by the team.*

- *Conrad, marketing's representative on the team. He will explain what has been learned about competing products and customer responses.*

- *Carliss, whose background is in financial management. She will use a set of computer-based slides to discuss the pro-forma sales costs associated with the new product line.*

You should allocate speakers either by their areas of expertise, as Samantha has done, or by their presentation strengths and weaknesses. For example, people with strong presentation skills are the best candidates for opening and closing the talk, when persuasiveness counts most. They can also be most effective during difficult time slots, such as before and after lunch and at the end of the day. If possible, arrange for a group rehearsal before the presentation so that each person is aware of what others are presenting.

Group presentation flow

What's the best way to integrate various contributors into a presentation? There is no single best way. However, a typical group presentation flows as follows:

- The first speaker introduces the other speakers briefly and introduces the topic.

- Each subsequent speaker provides a transition to the next one with a sentence: "Now June will cover . . ."

- The last speaker summarizes the whole presentation.

- A facilitator handles all transitions.

Visuals can pose logistical challenges for a group presentation. Extra planning can ensure that your visuals enhance your message rather than distract your audience. To make the most seamless presentation possible, follow these guidelines:

- Have someone other than the speaker handle the visuals during the presentation (unless the speaker prefers to do so).

- If someone else is handling the visuals, practice to achieve synchronization.

- Make sure that all slides or overheads follow the same format.

- If speakers are using different media, coordinate to make the transition smoothly.

Also, plan how the group will handle questions. Each speaker should be prepared to answer questions in a particular area and to follow up if another speaker needs help. If possible, avoid having every speaker comment on every question.

Rehearse

There are always three speeches for every
one you actually give. The one
you practice, the one you gave, and
the one you wish you gave.
—Dale Carnegie

W HEN WOULD YOU LIKE to learn about the holes, the dull spots, and excessive details in your presentation—before or after it's been delivered? Rehearse to find and repair these problems beforehand.

Effective rehearsing

To make the most of your rehearsal, practice your presentation on a test audience and get their feedback. Assemble people who are similar to your audience profile. For example, if you are presenting to experts on the topic, include an expert in your rehearsal audience and get that person's evaluation. Also, remember these tips:

- Rehearse with the equipment and visuals you will actually use at the event.

- Rehearse the entire presentation each time you practice.

- Rehearse out loud and, if possible, in front of a friend or colleague. Otherwise, practice with a tape or video recorder.

- Rehearse until the presentation does not sound memorized.

- Concentrate on the subject and your desire to communicate, not on your notes.

What Would YOU Do?

Prepared but Dull

BOB TURNS OFF THE videotape and shakes his head in frustration. How could his presentation have been so dull? He studied his audience, researched his subject, and worked for hours to develop a talk that was clear and concise. Now when he reviews the videotape, he notices some trouble spots. His head was buried in his notes, the audience seemed lost, and he came off as—well, not particularly charismatic. Bob knows he is actually pretty witty, outgoing, and even a good storyteller. He wonders how he can inject his own personality into a presentation so that he can better engage his audience. What would you do?

What You COULD Do.

In hindsight, Bob knows he could have done a number of things differently. For starters, he could have made more eye contact with the audience, used a conversational tone, and referred to his notes only when he needed to. He could also have prepared a few visuals to illustrate the key points of his talk. Visuals would have helped the audience stay focused. Finally, he could have incorporated relevant stories or examples that supported his material but didn't distract from his overall message. Implementing these measures next time will give Bob a more engaging and effective presentation.

Go the extra mile

Will this be a high-stakes presentation? If it will, go all out. If possible, conduct your rehearsal in the same room or hall where your presentation is scheduled. This will give you a sense of the room, your entryway and exit, and how loud you'll have to speak to reach the back row.

To make the most of your rehearsal, bring along a few objective colleagues. Place some in front, some in the middle, and others in the back row of seats. Then ask for feedback on your delivery and the effectiveness of the visual aids. Use the comments to bring the weak parts of the presentation up to a higher standard.

Prepare
Yourself

DELIVERING AN effective presentation requires mental preparation. Rehearsing your lines is one thing; putting yourself in the right state of mind before the curtain opens is another—and often as important.

Psych yourself

Fortunately, there are number of things you can do to win the mental game. Here are some examples:

- Visualize yourself giving a successful presentation. Repeat positive statements to yourself, such as, "I am relaxed and ready."

- Use breathing techniques and tension-relieving exercises to reduce stress.

- Ask yourself, "What's the worst that can happen?" Then be prepared for that possibility.

- Accept nervousness as natural, and do not try to counteract it with food, caffeine, drugs, or alcohol before the presentation.

Overcome fear

Many professional speakers, actors, and musical performers get a case of stage fright before going on, and yet they manage to get their fear in check. You must do the same. Consider the following tactics to help you overcome your fear:

- Rehearse your presentation, and know it well.

- Get to know audience members individually—by telephone before the presentation, or in person as they come into the room.

- Anticipate the questions and objections that are most likely to arise.

- Prepare physically and mentally.

Show
Time

Y OU'VE PREPARED YOUR messages, your materials, and yourself. You're now ready.

How to speak effectively

Once you're actually in the room with your audience, you must focus on delivering the most engaging presentation possible. You will achieve your best performance if you speak effectively, project a positive image, and keep your audience engaged. Here are some suggestions:

- Make your presentation conversational.

- Avoid the use of jargon or terms that may be unfamiliar to the audience.

- Watch the audience for nonverbal clues about their response.

- Breathe. It helps you relax and reduces filter language such as "um" and "er."

To use your voice to its best advantage, keep its tone natural and conversational. Speak loudly enough for everyone. In most cases, you can do this by speaking to the most distant person in the room. If you have a microphone and sound system, experiment with it when you rehearse. Here are a few more tips:

- Avoid rapid-fire or drawn-out speech. Practice with a tape recorder or a colleague to get feedback.

- Be expressive. Don't speak in a monotone. Raise and lower your voice to make your point.

- Enunciate and pronounce words clearly.

Project a positive image

Your confidence in and commitment to your message are reflected by your demeanor and body language. To optimize your effectiveness, make sure to do the following:

- Project confidence through your dress and presence.

- Make sure your facial expressions convey interest in the audience. If you are too nervous to look at the entire audience, focus on individuals instead.

- Make and maintain eye contact with audience members.

Techniques for keeping your audience engaged

Most speakers confront one or several difficult audience members: the tuned out, the overloaded, or people so busy that they are thinking about other pressing issues. People in these groups will not likely hear what you have to say unless you take measures to grab their attention and hold on to it.

But how can you tell which members of the audience are attentive and which are not? Psychologists say that people send nonverbal signals about their attentiveness. Those who are following what you say are busy watching you or your visuals, or they are busy taking notes. The inattentive cross their legs, fidget in their seats, or look around the room more than usual. Your challenge is to attract those wandering minds back to the presentation. Here are some proven techniques:

- Change what you're doing—for example, make a sudden pause or change your vocal tone.

- Ask for a show of hands: "Just out of curiosity, how many of you believe that your customers are satisfied with our current returns policy? Let's see a show of hands."

- Add humor. A little comic relief in a serious presentation is welcomed by audiences and captures their attention.

- Provide analogies and vivid examples.

- Introduce personal stories.

- Employ compelling statistics and expert testimony.

- Use visuals, such as illustrations, charts, and graphs, to good effect.

- Ask a question: "So what does that last point mean for you and your business?"

Tips for Presenting Effectively

- Do not talk from a script. Talk from notes.
- Face your audience and make eye contact.
- When you want control or more involvement, or to become one of the group, walk around your audience.
- Do not jingle keys or coins in your pockets.
- Use gestures in a relaxed and normal way.
- Use your voice effectively.
- Keep your focus on your message and your audience.

Questions taken from the audience can both engage the listeners and provide you with opportunities to furnish greater detail in areas that matter to your audience. However, it is important that you be well prepared for the questions you will receive.

Handling
Questions

QUESTIONS TAKEN FROM the audience can both engage the audience and provide you with opportunities to furnish greater detail in areas that matter to listeners. Some people feel that if there are no questions, the presentation is a success. However, if your listeners are engaged and are working with you, they most likely will have questions.

As part of your preparation, you should anticipate the questions most likely to be asked. You can do this if you understand your audience and its concerns.

The right time for Q&A

Many speakers take questions at the *end* of a presentation. This allows them to complete the talk within a specified time and be sure the audience has the whole picture. If you choose this approach, remember these tips:

- Make the transition to your Q&A session clear.

- Maintain control of the Q&A session by repeating the question and giving the answer to the whole group, not only to the questioner.

Some speakers also take questions *during* the presentation, thinking that it keeps people engaged and gives them immediate feedback about how well audience members understand the message. Use this approach with caution, because it may cause you to lose control of your talk.

Finally, other speakers take questions *at specific points* during the presentation. Such times might include when you want people's reactions or when you want their ideas. However, if you choose this approach, be sure to identify these points ahead of time and flag them in your presentation so that you do not forget to stop for questions.

Prepare yourself for the tough questions

Suppose you're presenting the company's new strategic plan to a group of anxious managers and employees. Or you're making a presentation to a group of executives and engineers from another company, with the goal of becoming a preferred supplier. Or the CEO has delegated you to go to each regional office to explain upcoming layoffs and related separation packages.

What do those presentations have in common? All are bound to evoke tough questions or objections from the audience. Q&A may be challenging, if not contentious. So before you give this type of presentation, prepare yourself for the tough questions that people are likely to ask. In many cases you can anticipate these questions if you put yourself in the shoes of your listeners.

Using the "Objections" worksheet, make a list of the tough questions or objections you anticipate. Once you have them on paper, develop a coherent response to each. Get help if you need it.

Objections

Complete this worksheet before your presentation to identify possible objections or issues that may be raised and prepare appropriate responses.

Audience Member/Group	Public Issues or Objections	Potential Responses (Acknowledge, Address, and Resolve)

When you don't have the answer

Even good preparation cannot anticipate every question. If you don't know the answer to a question, direct the person to a source for the answer or offer to get the answer.

Tips for Handling Questions

- If you know the answer, keep it clear and brief.
- If you don't know the answer to a question, direct the person to another source, offer to get the answer, or ask whether someone in the audience can answer the question.
- Anticipate questions and arguments. Don't deny or gloss over them.
- If questions are beginning to disrupt the flow of your presentation, record them on a whiteboard or flip chart and address them at the end of the meeting. ·

After-Action Review

LIKE OTHER ACTIVITIES, a speech or presentation is the result of a process that converts inputs (your ideas, information, and arguments) to outputs (what your audience sees and hears). And like every other process, it can be improved.

Find the root causes of problems

Process improvement—whether it has to do with making automobiles or making presentations to the sales group—is the foundation of quality. If you want better quality in your next presentation, examine the quality of the one you just delivered. Was it up to standards? Were there measurable defects, such as a slide that could not be read from the back of the room? When defects are found, trace them back to their root cause. Once the root causes are known, you can take corrective action.

If you take the time to objectively evaluate a presentation after its delivery (or after a rehearsal), you will be able to pinpoint the root causes of poor performance. For example, you may find cluttered overheads, weak opening remarks, inept attempts at humor, or something else. Once you've identified the problems, do something about them as you prepare for your next presentation.

A video can help

One of the best ways to evaluate your performance and to pinpoint areas for improvement is to videotape each presentation (or rehearsal) for later review. If this is not possible, ask one or more helpful colleagues to take note of what went well and what went poorly. An after-action review of the tape or the colleagues' notes will put you in touch with the best and worst of your presentation skills.

If you work on continuous improvement, your presentations will become more and more effective—and your standing in the organization will rise.

Tips and Tools

Tools for
Giving Presentations

Audience Characteristics

Use this worksheet as you prepare your presentation.

Question	Notes
1. Who are your listeners, and what is their relationship to your topic?	
2. How well informed are they about the subject matter?	
3. What do they need to know?	
4. What are their expectations of the larger event? Of your presentation?	
5. What do they know about you? What else might they need to know?	
6. What is their opinion of you or the organization you represent?	
7. Are they attending by choice or by requirement?	
8. Are they likely to be receptive? Enthusiastic? Polite? Hostile? Apathetic?	
9. Are there other obstacles, history, or expectations that you need to take into account?	
10. What presentation techniques might best capture their attention and get your points across most effectively (e.g., demonstrations, personal stories, multimedia)?	

Logistics

Complete this worksheet prior to your presentation to confirm that you haven't forgotten any of the logistical details.

Presentation Topic	
Date	
Presenter(s)	
Presentation Location	
Meeting Coordinator and Phone Number	
Site Contact Person and Phone Number	
Number of People Attending	
Handouts	

Room Setup

☐ Auditorium   ☐ Horseshoe   ☐ Podium

☐ Classroom   ☐ Breakout Sessions   ☐ Stage

☐ Conference   ☐ Tables: Front, Side, or Back

☐ Other:

Equipment and Supplies

☐ Computer(s)   ☐ Extension Cord(s)   ☐ Video equipment/ VCR player and monitors

☐ Overhead Projector/ Spare Bulbs   ☐ Flip Chart/Tape/ Markers   ☐ Phone Line(s)

☐ Projection Table   ☐ LCD Projector   ☐ Microphone

☐ Other:

Other

Presentation Context

Use this worksheet to better understand the context of your presentation.

Question	Notes
1. Is the presentation formal or informal?	
2. When you present, will the audience have just finished eating, drinking, working, or doing something active?	
3. Who will speak before and after you? What do they plan to say?	
4. Are you the first or last speaker of the program? The day? The morning or afternoon?	
5. Are you expected to answer questions or leave copies of your presentation?	
6. How much time do you have for the presentation? Can your message be delivered in that time? If not, can it be adapted and still be effective?	
7. Will the physical setting of the room require you to adapt your presentation in any way?	

Preliminary Planning

Use this worksheet to help you plan the content of your presentation.

Topic

Requested by

Objectives

If your presentation is a success, what will be the immediate results?

Main Messages

What must the audience understand and remember from your presentation?

1.

2.

3.

4.

5.

Supporting Facts

What facts support your main messages?

Message 1

Message 2

Message 3

Message 4

Message 5

Presentation Outline

Use this worksheet to help you organize your content most effectively, identify any visuals or support materials that will enhance your presentation, and estimate the time you will need. You may have to revise your content if it appears to exceed your time limitations.

Your Content	Visuals/Support Materials	Time
Opening • State your purpose. • Preview your main points. • Make your audience want to listen.		
Body • Get across the main points of your presentation.		
Conclusion • Summarize your content. • Challenge the audience to take action.		

Objections

Complete this worksheet before your presentation to identify possible objections or issues that may be raised and prepare appropriate responses.

Audience Member/Group	Public Issues or Objections	Potential Responses (Acknowledge, Address, and Resolve)

Test Yourself

This section offers ten multiple-choice questions to help you see what you've learned and identify areas that you might want to explore further. The answers are found at the end of this section.

1. Which of the following is not a recommended strategy to help you prepare yourself mentally and physically to make a presentation?

    a. Visualizing yourself giving a successful presentation; repeating to yourself positive statements, such as, "I am relaxed and ready."

    b. Psyching yourself up for successful speaking.

    c. Not accepting being nervous and trying to counteract your nervousness using any means possible.

2. The type of presentation you choose depends on which of the following?

    a. How formal the presentation will be.

    b. Who will attend, what you want to say, and how you should say it.

    c. The size of the audience that can attend.

3. When you are considering what will help you accomplish the objectives of your presentation, what is one of the most important "do not" guidelines to remember?

   a. Do not speak spontaneously; use notes.

   b. Do not talk just about facts.

   c. Do not describe the outcome you hope will result after the presentation.

4. Most experts agree that it is important to limit the number of messages and main ideas covered in a single presentation. What is this generally agreed-upon limit?

   a. Three.

   b. Five.

   c. Nine.

5. The opening of a presentation has four parts: (1) describing the importance of the topic for the audience, (2) establishing your credibility, and (3) previewing the main points to be covered. What is the fourth part?

   a. Including clear statements of the main points.

   b. Defining the purpose of the presentation.

   c. Distributing all related supporting materials.

6. During the body of a presentation, what is an effective way to involve the audience?

    a. Ask the audience for suggestions and questions.

    b. Add visual aids, such as overheads, to support your main messages.

    c. Pass out a sheet on which the audience can note questions about the content to use during the final Q&A session.

7. How long should a presentation be?

    a. In general, not more than one to one and a half hours.

    b. Any length, as long as you make several points and cover them in detail.

    c. As long as it needs to be to convey at least one message clearly and completely.

8. When is an appropriate time to distribute handouts during a presentation?

    a. Before, during, or after the presentation, depending on your objectives.

    b. During the presentation.

    c. Either before the presentation or after it.

9. What aspects of a presentation are the most effective in making the messages and desired outcome most persuasive?

    a. Expert testimony, statistics, visual aids such as charts and graphs, and audience involvement.

    b. Personal stories, examples, humor, and analogies.

    c. Enthusiasm, credibility, and personal belief in the subject.

10. What is an effective way to handle a question when you don't have the answer?

    a. Get the individual's name, write down the question, and ask the questioner to talk with you at the end of the presentation. Don't, however, state that you don't know.

    b. First, indicate that it's a good question. Admit you don't know the answer, and then move on to the next question.

    c. Direct the person to a source or offer to get the answer, or ask whether someone in the audience can answer the question.

Answers to test questions

1, c. Not accepting being nervous and trying to counteract your nervousness using any means possible.

You should accept nervousness as natural. Trying to counteract it by consuming drugs, caffeine, or alcohol before your presentation will likely have a negative effect on your delivery. However, visualizing a successful presentation and psyching yourself up can help you prepare mentally.

2, b. Who will attend, what you want to say, and how you should say it.

The type of presentation you choose depends on your purpose for the meeting. After you select the appropriate type, it's important to take into account the size of the audience, the formality of the situation, and the regularity of the meeting.

3, b. Do not talk just about facts.

Although facts are important to support your ideas and therefore your objective, it's important to remember that facts are seldom ends in themselves. In addition, including too many facts can create information overload. Limit the number of facts you present and avoid excessive detail.

4, b. Five.

Try to limit your message and main ideas to no more than five. Five, plus or minus two, seems to be the memory limit of most adults for recalling important messages. And the more complex your message, the smaller the number should be.

5, b. Defining the purpose of the presentation.

The fourth component is defining the purpose of the presentation in clear, concise language. It is actually the first thing you want to tell your audience.

6, a. Ask the audience for suggestions and questions.

Involving the audience by asking for their suggestions and then addressing their needs and issues makes the presentation truly interactive.

7, c. As long as it needs to be to convey at least one message clearly and completely.

Equally important when you consider length is to complete the meeting within the allocated time. Remember, if you don't have time to make a point clear or acceptable to your audience, save it for another presentation.

8, c. Either before the presentation or after it.

For the best results, distribute handouts either before the presentation, with enough time for people to absorb the content before you speak, or after, so that the audience has a summary of your key points to review.

9, c. Enthusiasm, credibility, and personal belief in the subject.

Your persuasiveness is largely a product of those qualities. Using arguments that combine logic and emotion can make your entire presentation more persuasive. Other options, such as expert testimony, visual aids, personal stories, statistics, examples, and so on, do make it more interesting and compelling.

10, c. Direct the person to a source or offer to get the answer, or ask whether someone in the audience can answer the question.

It's important not to avoid, deny, or gloss over any question or argument.

To Learn More

Articles

Ballaro, Beverly. "Six Ways to Grab Your Audience from the Start." *Harvard Management Communication Letter*, June 2003.

The most compelling information in the world won't make it through to most of your audience unless you convey it in a compelling way. To grab—and keep—your audience's attention, it is critical to make a powerful connection at the outset. Read the six tips offered by experts that will help you increase the receptivity of your message, whether it is spoken or written.

Harvard Business School Publishing. "Are Your Presentations Inspiring?" *Harvard Management Communications Letter,* January 2001.

Few presentations manage to say the right thing succinctly. One exception was John F. Kennedy's speech to the citizens of West Berlin in June 1963. This analysis of that speech reveals six lessons for any manager who wants to make an impact on an audience: (1) write the speech yourself; (2) keep it simple and true; (3) meet audience needs; (4) appeal to something larger than self-interest; (5) identify with the audience early on; and (6) repeat memorable phrases often.

Morgan, Nick. "Preparing to Be Real." *Harvard Management Communication Letter*, January 2004.

Rehearsal is more than learning lines and practicing gestures; it's a critical business skill. Why do businesspeople forgo rehearsal, in spite of overwhelming evidence that winging it is not a good idea? It's because most of them are so nervous about public speaking that they prefer to put off everything about it as long as possible rather than confront their fears. The good news is that with a little forethought, preparation, and—yes—rehearsal, you can deliver a presentation that connects with your audience.

Morgan, Nick. "Opening Options: How to Grab Your Audience's Attention." *Harvard Management Communication Letter*, July 2003.

The beginning moments of any presentation are the most difficult to create and deliver. Audiences make up their minds about you within the first minute or two; the pressure is always on. So how do you get started? Read these six interesting ways to get your presentation started on the right foot.

Sandberg, Kirsten. "Easy on the Eyes." *Harvard Management Communication Letter*, August 2002.

In this lively Q&A, renowned graphic designer Nigel Holmes offers his views on how graphics are used to convey information. In addition to sketching out best practices for creating charts and presentation graphics, he ruminates on a variety of related themes, including the way people take in visual information and the role and influence of PowerPoint in business.

Wiles, Cheryl. "Take Your Speech Cues from the Actor's Trade." *Harvard Management Communications Letter,* August 2004.

Do you suffer from stage fright when giving a presentation? If you begin to think of communication as an art, the way actors do, you'll improve your ability to speak before a crowd. Study the techniques actors use to enhance speaking skills, and you'll soon command more attention.

Books

Harvard Business School Publishing. *The Manager's Guide to Effective Presentations II.* Harvard Management Communication Letter Collection. Boston: Harvard Business School Publishing, 2000.

This collection from the pages of the *Harvard Management Communication Letter* offers time-tested tips for maximizing the impact of your presentations.

Morgan, Nick. *Working the Room: How to Move People to Action Through Audience-Centered Speaking.* Boston: Harvard Business School Press, 2003.

Do you remember the topic of the last speech you heard? If not, you're not alone. In fact, studies show that audiences remember only 10 to 30 percent of speech or presentation content. Given those bleak statistics, why do we give speeches at all? We give them, says communications expert Nick Morgan, because they remain the most powerful way of connecting with audiences. In this book, Morgan offers an audience-centered approach to public speaking. Through insightful examples, Morgan illustrates a three-part process—focusing on content development, rehearsal, and delivery—that will enable readers of all experience levels to give more effective, passion-filled speeches.

Morrisey, George L., Thomas Sechrest, and Wendy B. Warman. *Loud and Clear: How to Prepare and Deliver Effective Business and Technical Presentations.* Reading, MA: Addison-Wesley Publishing Company, 1997.

This book is a concise guide to all aspects of preparing and delivering a typical business presentation. In addition to guidelines and advice, the book contains a number of useful forms to help presenters get organized.

Sources for Giving Presentations

Harvard Business School Publishing. *Business Communication.* Boston: Harvard Business School Press, 2003.

Morrisey, George L., Thomas Sechrest, and Wendy B. Warman. *Loud and Clear: How to Prepare and Deliver Effective Business and Technical Presentations.* Reading, MA: Addison-Wesley Publishing Company, 1997.

Notes

How to Order

Harvard Business School Press publications are available world-wide from your local bookseller or online retailer.

You can also call:
1-800-668-6780

Our product consultants are available to help you 8:00 a.m.–6:00 p.m., Monday–Friday, Eastern Time. Outside the U.S. and Canada, call: 617-783-7450.

Please call about special discounts for quantities greater than ten.

You can order online at:
www.HBSPress.org